Frameworks for Assessment of USEUCOM Efforts to Inform, Influence, and Persuade

MIRIAM MATTHEWS, CHRISTOPHER PAUL, DAVID SCHULKER,
DAVID STEBBINS

Prepared for the United States European Command
Approved for public release; distribution unlimited

NATIONAL DEFENSE RESEARCH INSTITUTE

For more information on this publication, visit www.rand.org/t/RR2998

Library of Congress Cataloging-in-Publication Data is available for this publication.
ISBN: 978-1-9774-0524-1

Published by the RAND Corporation, Santa Monica, Calif.
© Copyright 2020 RAND Corporation
RAND® is a registered trademark.

Cover images: Adobe Stock

Support RAND
Make a tax-deductible charitable contribution at
www.rand.org/giving/contribute

www.rand.org

Preface

To achieve key national security objectives, the U.S. Department of Defense and other U.S. government organizations must effectively and credibly inform, influence, and persuade a broad range of foreign audiences. And to ensure that finite resources are allocated appropriately, that plans can be refined, and that key objectives can be realized, it is important to accurately and consistently assess the progress, performance, and effectiveness of these programs and activities. Unfortunately, designing and implementing such assessments can be challenging.

This report supports U.S. European Command's (USEUCOM's) information staff (ECJ39) and related inter- and intraorganizational partners in their various assessment design efforts. It describes, in detail, several evaluation and monitoring frameworks for USEUCOM's current and future efforts to inform, influence, and persuade various audiences. The frameworks are specifically designed to support and complement existing processes used by ECJ39. The report also provides guidance on the design of planned and ongoing efforts as a way to help ECJ39 evaluate and monitor influence activities. Although the primary audience is ECJ39 and USEUCOM personnel, this report will also likely be of interest to USEUCOM's inter- and intraorganizational partners, such as the regional service component commands, the U.S. Department of State, allied nations' militaries and ministries of defense, and North Atlantic Treaty Organization formations and commands. Personnel in other geographic combatant commands and members of the broader defense community who are tasked with evaluating efforts to inform, influence, and persuade should also find elements of this report useful and enlightening.

This research was sponsored by USEUCOM and conducted within the International Security and Defense Policy Center of the RAND National Defense Research Institute, a federally funded research and development center sponsored by the Office of the Secretary of Defense, the Joint Staff, the Unified Combatant Commands, the Navy, the Marine Corps, the defense agencies, and the defense intelligence enterprise.

For more information on the RAND International Security and Defense Policy Center, see www.rand.org/nsrd/isdp or contact the director (contact information is provided on the webpage).

Contents

Figures and Table

Figures

Table

Summary

The ability to effectively and credibly communicate with and influence a broad range of foreign audiences is critical to achieving key U.S. national security objectives. The U.S. Department of Defense (DoD) and other U.S. government organizations also need the capability to accurately and consistently measure the progress, performance, and effectiveness of programs and activities that are intended to inform, influence, and persuade these audiences to ensure that finite resources are allocated appropriately, that plans can be refined, and that key objectives are realized. Unfortunately, designing and implementing such assessments can be challenging.

The guidance and recommendations in this report are intended to support the assessment design efforts of U.S. European Command's (USEUCOM's) information staff (ECJ39). However, they are also likely to be useful to related inter- and intra-organizational partners, including other USEUCOM staff sections, regional service component commands, the U.S. Department of State, allied nations' militaries and ministries of defense, and North Atlantic Treaty Organization formations and commands.

In providing assistance to ECJ39, we developed a series of evaluation and monitoring frameworks for the command's current and future efforts to inform, influence, and persuade audiences. We also prepared guidance to support the design of planned and ongoing evaluation and monitoring efforts. To ensure that our frameworks and guidance met the needs of ECJ39 and USEUCOM, we interviewed ECJ39 and USEUCOM stakeholders and invited a larger group to participate in a multiday workshop to discuss measurement design and implementation. A separate RAND document includes the lexicon for discussing the measurement of influence efforts and serves as a helpful companion to this report.[1]

---

[1] Christopher Paul and Miriam Matthews, *The Language of Inform, Influence, and Persuade: Assessment Lexicon and Usage Guide for U.S. European Command Efforts*, Santa Monica, Calif.: RAND Corporation, RR-2655-EUCOM, 2018. This project also produced documentation, provided directly to USEUCOM stakeholders, that applied the frameworks described in this report to specific ECJ39 efforts.

Development and Implementation of a Progress Assessment Framework

Progress assessment is a type of assessment activity that measures movement toward one or more objectives, whether that movement is due to intentional efforts, unintentional efforts, or changes in context.[2] Thus, the measurement of progress toward an objective might consider the contributions of more than one program or effort. Numerous operations, activities, and investments (OAIs) might be undertaken in pursuit of a single goal or objective, and a commander, sponsor, or other stakeholder might want an overall measurement of progress rather than a detailed understanding of the individual contributions of each line of effort (LOE). In other words, a senior leader might want to know about overall advancement toward an objective across multiple OAIs.

Progress assessment is a feedback process and part of a larger planning and execution loop. The first step in progress assessment is to identify the goals or objectives toward which progress will be assessed—typically a subset of an effort's goals and objectives. Organizations and units often rely on laws, regulations, guidance on policies and strategies, and leadership priorities to establish objectives.

Within USEUCOM, large sets of objectives drawn from guidance, theater priorities, and LOEs can help identify which subordinate objectives, or sub-objectives, are most relevant to a progress assessment (see Figure S.1). After candidate sub-objectives are identified, final selections are made in consultation with appropriate stakeholders.

Figure S.1
Progress Assessment Framework

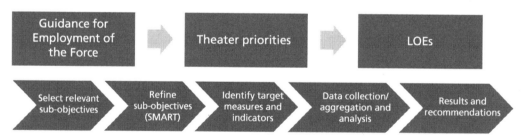

NOTE: Guidance for Employment of the Force is used primarily for planning and can inform theater priorities, which inform LOEs. *Refine sub-objectives (SMART)* refers to the process of refining sub-objectives to ensure that they are specific, measurable, achievable, relevant, and time-bound. At the time of this research, plans were underway to replace Guidance for Employment of the Force with the Global Force Management Allocation Plan and Global Force Management Implementation Guidance.

---

[2]   Paul and Matthews, 2018.

After selecting relevant sub-objectives, ECJ39 must begin to refine them.[3] Joint Publication (JP) 5-0, *Joint Planning*, describes objectives as "clearly defined, decisive, and attainable goals toward which every operation is directed" that are, ideally, "specific, measurable, achievable, relevant, and time-bound," or *SMART*.[4] If selected sub-objectives are not SMART, ECJ39 will need to make refinements to measure progress against them.

After receiving requisite feedback and refining selected sub-objectives, ECJ39 should identify target measures and indicators. What information to capture should be determined through a two-step process. The first step is to identify what information is needed to address questions regarding progress made. This could involve identifying possible proxy measures for SMART sub-objectives or, if sub-objectives have needed refinement, identifying proxy measures for measures of effectiveness (MOEs). In this step, the focus should be on determining what information and data might be needed, not on creating needs that might be addressed by currently collected data. In other words, the selected sub-objectives should drive identification of measures and indicators, not the other way around. Collecting and analyzing measures and indicators that do not fully address a construct of interest and attempting to use them to assess progress toward multiple, wide-ranging sub-objectives could limit the utility of any resulting assessment, perpetuate knowledge gaps, and create confusion. However, it is important to note that all data collection is bound by resource and capability constraints and burdens on staff; these limitations will likely influence which measures or indicators can be obtained, making stakeholder and leadership engagement during the measure or indicator identification process particularly worthwhile.

After identification, target measures and indicators should be collected and analyzed, possibly using aggregation techniques. To address progress, or change, one option is for analysts to examine changes observed in the measures or indicators over time, a process known as *longitudinal data analysis*. This longitudinal analysis can begin with a baseline assessment, which provides information about a location or context before the implementation of a particular OAI. If there is ongoing data collection addressing the location or context of interest, the collected data and results might be able to provide this initial information.

Choosing relevant sub-objectives and addressing them using collected data on identified target measures will help ensure that the resulting analysis provides useful insights. Sharing draft recommendations that map the results to potential next steps or additional actions can help communicate these insights as they are collected and give stakeholders an opportunity to provide feedback or make changes to the OAI. In prac-

---

[3] Note that, formally, the objectives should be refined after sub-objectives have been selected and approved by relevant stakeholders. In practice, initial refinement could occur in conjunction with the selection process, though it can be completed only after sub-objective selections are finalized.

[4] JP 5-0, *Joint Planning*, Washington, D.C.: U.S. Joint Chiefs of Staff, June 16, 2017, p. I-10.

tice, these draft recommendations might be developed by ECJ39 leadership and relevant working groups, including working groups that address measures and indicators, effects development, relevant LOEs, and joint effects. These working groups might change over time, such that groups may be created, combined, or abolished, so ECJ39 will need to monitor which working groups are appropriate to address the attributes of interest as the progress assessment process unfolds. Each of the identified working groups should review the results and develop or modify recommendations. This feedback should then inform subsequent actions and plans.

A Framework for Performance Assessment and Effectiveness Assessment

To understand overall advancement toward an objective, an individual or organization may request or conduct a progress assessment (as described previously) that can incorporate measures from multiple OAIs. However, for a more thorough understanding of a single OAI's functioning or contribution to overall progress, a performance assessment in conjunction with an *effectiveness assessment* fits the bill. Performance assessments and effectiveness assessments can be considered subordinate to progress assessments: Multiple performance and effectiveness assessments might be incorporated into a progress assessment. Specifically, performance and effectiveness assessments can provide information that could be used in a broader progress assessment that addresses overall advancement toward at least one objective.[5] A performance assessment provides feedback regarding the extent or quality of the implementation of one OAI, and it includes measures of performance (MOPs).[6] An effectiveness assessment addresses the contribution of one OAI to the advancement toward a goal or objective, and it includes MOEs and MOE indicators (MOEIs).[7]

Objectives provide the foundation for measuring progress, performance, and effectiveness. For example, to implement a progress assessment, an organization—with input from its stakeholders—must select relevant sub-objectives, such as a theater priority from guidance documents. After they are selected, the sub-objectives should be refined, as needed, to ensure that they are SMART. These refined sub-objectives

---

[5] Paul and Matthews, 2018.

[6] JP 5-0 (2017) defines an MOP as "[a]n indicator used to measure a friendly action that is tied to measuring task accomplishment" (p. GL-12).

[7] JP 5-0 (2017) defines an MOE as "[a]n indicator used to measure a current system state, with change indicated by comparing multiple observations over time" (p. GL-12). It does not define *MOEI*, but JP 3-13 describes such indicators as "a unit, location, or event observed or measured, that can be used to assess an MOE. These are often used to add quantitative data points to qualitative MOEs and can assist an IO [information operations] staff or IO cell in answering a question related to a qualitative MOE" (JP 3-13, *Information Operations*, Washington, D.C.: U.S. Joint Chiefs of Staff, November 27, 2012, incorporating change 1, November 20, 2014, p. IV-10).

inform the identification of target measures and indicators for the broader progress assessment. These refined sub-objectives should also inform the development and implementation of individual OAIs, which can be monitored and evaluated through the use of more-specific performance assessments and effectiveness assessments (see Figure S.2). In other words, the refined sub-objectives developed during the progress assessment process can inform the performance and effectiveness assessment processes.

Selected and refined sub-objectives should inform the joint operation planning process or other process that shapes a particular OAI. These planning processes involve several steps.[8] After appropriate authorities recognize a need for military activities (e.g., as planning begins or a mission is received), commanders and strategists must analyze the operational environment. Drawing from selected and refined sub-objectives, they should determine the desired future state of this operational environment (e.g., through mission analysis or problem framing). After that, possible courses of action (COAs) can be developed, analyzed, and compared with selected criteria. This should

Figure S.2
Performance Assessment and Effectiveness Assessment Framework

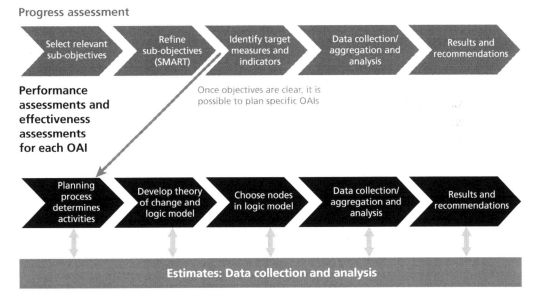

NOTE: Measures from multiple performance and effectiveness assessments across relevant OAIs can inform the broader progress assessment. Estimates can be used if necessary.

---

[8]   Center for Army Lessons Learned, *MDMP: Lessons and Best Practices*, No. 15-06, March 2015; JP 3-30, *Joint Air Operations*, Washington, D.C.: U.S. Joint Chiefs of Staff, July 25, 2019; Headquarters, U.S. Department of the Army, *Psychological Operations Leaders Planning Guide*, Graphic Training Aid 33-01-001, November 2005; Curtis E. Lemay Center for Doctrine Development and Education, *The Joint Operation Planning Process for Air*, November 4, 2016.

occur before requesting commander approval and developing a detailed plan for the approved COA (e.g., plan or order development or order production, dissemination, and transition).

After COAs have been established, ECJ39 should develop a theory of change for each relevant OAI. If a theory of change already exists for a similar effort, ECJ39 could draw from that and tailor it to the new effort. A theory of change describes the connections among resources, activities, contextual factors, and outcomes. It also identifies how the planned elements of an effort will achieve specific objectives, thereby making implicit assumptions regarding processes more explicit.[9] A logic model is a visualization tool that can assist with developing a theory of change. Note that specification of the end state to be achieved (ends), actions to achieve that end state (ways), and resources required to take those actions (means) is a common military process and similar to articulating a theory of change.

After developing a theory of change and logic model, ECJ39 should determine which nodes within the logic model to measure. It will likely not be possible to measure all elements and connections in the model; fortunately, it is not always necessary to measure everything. Not all nodes address fundamental assumptions or uncertainties, and attempting to measure everything can be costly in terms of time, personnel, and money.[10] When deciding what to measure, the logic model can illustrate which candidate measures address core components, vulnerable assumptions, and critical uncertainties. Priority should be given to measuring parts of the logic model that address core cause-and-effect relationships and uncertain assumptions, as well as those that could provide a clear picture of success or failure (as opposed to strictly prioritizing indicators of success).

In the next step of the process, data collection, analysis, and aggregation can occur. Measures identified in the previous step can be used to evaluate changes over time. However, this often requires a baseline measurement of the conditions or context of interest. Currently collected estimates might provide baseline measurements before OAI implementation.

ECJ39 should provide regular, brief updates to working groups on effects development and LOEs or other stakeholders. These updates can incorporate both clear and concise summaries of results and explicit descriptions that clarify the relevance of the results for the OAI of interest. The frequency with which these updates are provided and to whom they should be given can be determined through discussion and coordination with stakeholders.

---

[9]   Christopher Paul, Jessica Yeats, Colin P. Clarke, Miriam Matthews, and Lauren Skrabala, *Assessing and Evaluating Department of Defense Efforts to Inform, Influence, and Persuade: Handbook for Practitioners*, Santa Monica, Calif.: RAND Corporation, RR-809/2-OSD, 2015.

[10]   Christopher Paul, *Assessing and Evaluating Department of Defense Efforts to Inform, Influence, and Persuade: Worked Example*, Santa Monica, Calif.: RAND Corporation, RR-809/4-OSD, 2017.

Framework Application: Addressing the Effects of Major Coalition Exercises

ECJ39 planners face multiple challenges in attempting to design performance and effectiveness assessments for USEUCOM OAIs, particularly in the case of resource-intensive military exercises that can involve one or more partner nations. These exercises are often large and complex. They can demand multiple capabilities, and there may be varying levels of interoperability between U.S. and partner forces. Discerning the contribution of such activities to various objectives (including foreign policy objectives) is inherently difficult. A second challenge is that USEUCOM exercises might intend to affect future adversary decisions by shaping adversary perceptions—an objective that is fraught with imperfect knowledge and measurement limitations. Deterring adversaries from engaging in unwanted behaviors, for example, requires understanding the inputs to adversary perceptions that make alternative behaviors more attractive.[11] The complexity of adversary motivations regarding aggression, the difficulty of observing shifts in such motivations over time, and the potential influence of external factors can limit the capabilities of effectiveness assessments.[12] Finally, it is not always possible to establish causal links between what a military exercise seeks to affect (such as partner investments in capabilities or adversary deterrence) and a subsequent behavior. In terms of deterrence, for example, it is likely impossible to determine definitively that an adversary has decided to be aggressive or show restraint as a result of a particular USEUCOM exercise.

To this end, commanders must weigh COAs based on some criteria (formal or informal) for what will be most effective. The challenge facing USEUCOM planners, then, is to continuously refine assessment structures so that they incrementally improve the quality of the information provided to commanders.

ECJ39 planners often inherit high-level objectives that lack SMART attributes, making the objectives difficult to assess. The first way that ECJ39 planners can improve the design of different types of assessments—even in a challenging environment—is to work toward refining sub-objectives. This includes specifying target audiences for each message, desired behaviors for partners and adversaries, and the time horizon for expected effects.

The next step in designing comprehensive performance and effectiveness assessments is to fully enumerate the theory of change. Grounding measurement plans in an explicit theory of change represented in a logic model can provide important feedback for commanders. For example, these designs can help commanders distinguish

---

[11] Michael J. Mazarr, *Understanding Deterrence*, Santa Monica, Calif.: RAND Corporation, PE-295-RC, 2018.

[12] John Gale, Stephenie Loux, and Andrew Coburn, *Creating Program Logic Models: A Toolkit for State Flex Programs*, Minneapolis, Minn., Chapel Hill, N.C., and Portland, Me.: Flex Monitoring Team, University of Minnesota, University of North Carolina, and University of Southern Maine, April 2006.

between program failure and theory failure. If metrics indicate that inputs were in place, activities were executed appropriately, and the outputs of interest were achieved but the outcomes of interest were not realized, then this would suggest theory failure. By contrast, if input and output metrics suggest that a program was not implemented as intended, then this would suggest program failure.

Recommendations

The following recommendations are intended to guide the actions and considerations of planners and practitioners:

- ECJ39 and working groups within USEUCOM should adopt the frameworks and processes for assessment design and implementation described in this report. This will help ensure that planners and practitioners address the core components of an OAI whenever senior leadership requires a progress, performance, or effectiveness assessment.
- Planners and assessment practitioners should begin an assessment design by defining or refining sub-objectives that are SMART.
- Planners and assessment practitioners should engage relevant stakeholders throughout the assessment design process.
- Measures and indicators should clearly address identified objectives and underlying theories of change.
- When communicating results, assessment practitioners should include information about the intent of the data collection and analysis, along with recommendations for how specific stakeholders can use results.
- Commanders should recognize that high-quality assessment design requires time and resources and ensure that assessment planners and practitioners have sufficient time and resources to implement well-designed progress, performance, and effectiveness assessments.

Acknowledgments

We thank the various personnel in ECJ39, their supporting contractors, and personnel from other staff sections who participated in a May 2018 assessment workshop and provided us with valuable background. We particularly benefited from insights from Colonel Mike Jackson, Major Wonny Kim, Eric Damm, James "Mags" Maggelet, Erin Weisgerber, and Austin Branch.

Abbreviations

COA	course of action
DoD	U.S. Department of Defense
DO JOC	Deterrence Operations Joint Operating Concept
ECJ39	U.S. European Command information staff
IE	information environment
IO	information operations
ISR	intelligence, surveillance, and reconnaissance
J3	operations directorate
J5	strategy, plans, and policy directorate
J5/8	strategy, policy, programs, and resources directorate
J7	joint force development directorate
JP	joint publication
LOE	line of effort
MOE	measure of effectiveness
MOEI	measure of effectiveness indicator
MOP	measure of performance
NATO	North Atlantic Treaty Organization
OAI	operation, activity, or investment
SMART	specific, measurable, achievable, relevant, and time-bound

TCO   theater campaign order

USEUCOM   U.S. European Command

CHAPTER ONE

Introduction

Across both the public and private sectors, the ideal is to make evidence-based decisions based on the extent to which a particular effort is meeting one or more common goals, but this is not possible without systematic data collection and analysis.[1] Measuring advancement toward a goal or objective is a priority in the U.S. Department of Defense (DoD) and is directly relevant to efforts to inform, influence, and persuade various audiences.[2] For example, Joint Publication (JP) 3-13, *Information Operations*, dedicates an entire chapter to assessment and states, "Assessment of IO [information operations] is a key component of the commander's decision cycle, helping to determine the results of tactical actions in the context of overall mission objectives and providing potential recommendations for refinement of future plans."[3] This statement highlights the utility of data and analysis in informing subsequent decisions and actions, specifically those involving operations in the information environment (IE). In particular, the progress, performance, and effectiveness of operations, activities, and investments (OAIs) that are aimed at informing, influencing, and persuading others must be measured accurately and consistently so that they can be refined, finite resources can be allocated efficiently, and advancement toward key objectives can be reported to commanders and other stakeholders. Unfortunately, designing and implementing different types of assessments of these influence-related efforts can be challenging.

One difficulty that planners must address is that influence efforts often seek to affect human perception and cognition—specifically, attitudes and opinions. Yet, it is difficult to observe and measure these "cognitive dimensions" accurately and consistently. Rather than strictly addressing attitudes and opinions, some influence efforts

---

seek to affect audience *behaviors*. A change in behavior is more easily observable and measurable than a shift in attitude or opinion, but causal conflation can hinder the interpretation of collected behavioral data. In other words, differentiating between the impact of a particular influence effort and the effects of other exogenous factors can be problematic.

Even when there is satisfactory measurement at a granular level, meaningfully aggregating different types of measures to compare the relative merits of a particular effort or to create a composite picture of overall progress toward a campaign-level objective can be an additional challenge. For example, at any time, various U.S. government and military offices and task forces are engaged in influence activities, sometimes in support of the same objective. Questions regarding the extent to which each activity is contributing to overall progress, if at all, can be difficult to answer. Therefore, the planners must grapple with how to accurately and concisely address queries regarding the effects of individual activities with the same or similar goals.

The best evaluations show trends over time and draw on valid and reliable measures collected consistently over the duration of an OAI. However, objectives can change before, during, and after implementation, or the personnel who are responsible for designing and implementing the effort might move to new assignments. This can make it difficult to consistently measure influence efforts and overall progress toward a campaign objective. Effective frameworks for assessments need to be flexible enough to allow for changing missions and circumstances but sufficiently enduring to retain their validity despite these changes.

This report is part of a RAND project to support U.S. European Command (USEUCOM) in accurately assessing its influence efforts. In providing this assistance, we developed evaluation and monitoring frameworks for the command's current and future efforts to inform, influence, and persuade audiences and provided additional guidance for designing assessments. Thus, the primary intended audience for this report is USEUCOM and related inter- and intraorganizational partners, including other USEUCOM staff sections, regional component commands, the U.S. Department of State, allied nations' militaries and ministries of defense, and North Atlantic Treaty Organization (NATO) formations and commands. Personnel in other geographic combatant commands or the broader defense community who are tasked with evaluating efforts to inform, influence, and persuade might also find the report informative. A separate RAND document includes the lexicon for discussing the measurement of influence efforts and serves as a helpful companion to this report.[4]

---

[4]   Christopher Paul and Miriam Matthews, *The Language of Inform, Influence, and Persuade: Assessment Lexicon and Usage Guide for U.S. European Command Efforts*, Santa Monica, Calif.: RAND Corporation, RR-2655-EUCOM, 2018. This project also produced documentation, provided directly to USEUCOM stakeholders, that applied the frameworks described in this report to specific ECJ39 efforts.

Research Approach

To develop appropriate frameworks and provide specific guidance to USEUCOM, we visited the command and its supporting components (e.g., U.S. Marine Forces Europe and Africa) to discuss recent, current, and ongoing USEUCOM efforts to inform, influence, and persuade, as well as related evaluation and monitoring efforts. We specifically engaged with USEUCOM's information staff (ECJ39) and assessment personnel to ascertain their needs and requirements for monitoring, measuring, and evaluating these efforts. This engagement included identifying the stakeholders and types of decisions that ECJ39 and assessment personnel support, along with the type of information required to meet these needs. We also participated in a multiday workshop that included in-depth discussion of the design and implementation of relevant USEUCOM measurement efforts.

The research process involved reviewing relevant strategy documents, briefings, and other USEUCOM documentation to better understand how the command's inform, influence, and persuade efforts support and relate to higher-level internal and broader DoD guidance and strategy, including the USEUCOM theater campaign plan and theater campaign order (TCO). Drawing on previous research on assessment and evaluation, we identified opportunities for USEUCOM to enhance its measurement and monitoring practices and developed robust but flexible frameworks to guide its assessment processes. Finally, we identified potential gaps in USEUCOM's ability to implement and execute the proposed frameworks and offered recommendations for addressing them.

Organization of This Report

The remainder of this report presents frameworks and guidance that USEUCOM can use to support its assessment of efforts to inform, influence, and persuade. Chapter Two describes a framework for measuring overall progress toward an objective and the contributions of individual OAIs. Chapter Three describes a framework for measuring the performance and effectiveness of these individual efforts. Chapter Four illustrates how to apply the frameworks described in Chapters Two and Three to efforts of interest to ECJ39. Chapter Five reprises core findings and presents our recommendations.

CHAPTER TWO

A Framework for Developing and Implementing Progress Assessments

Progress assessment is a type of assessment activity that measures movement toward one or more objectives, whether that movement is intentional, unintentional, or a result of changes in context.[1] Thus, a progress assessment might need to consider the contributions of more than one OAI. Numerous efforts might be undertaken in pursuit of the same goal or objective, and a commander or other senior leader might want to know the overall progress toward that goal or objective across OAIs and may not need a detailed understanding of the individual contributions of each effort.

A progress assessment is the application of systematic methods to address questions regarding the extent to which one or more objectives have been achieved or met. It first requires an objective against which advancement can be measured. A progress assessment can include multiple, complex OAIs, provided they all contribute to the identified objective. It might also consider the impact of the actions of others, chance events, or global trends. Within DoD, specifically, examples of progress assessment include campaign assessments or operation assessments. In this chapter, we present a framework for developing and implementing progress assessments, focusing on its possible application in the context of USEUCOM ECJ39 efforts.

Identifying Progress Assessment Objectives from Guidance and Priorities

Progress assessment is a feedback process and part of a larger planning and execution loop. The first step is to identify relevant priorities, goals, or objectives toward which progress will be assessed; these are likely a subset of the goals and objectives pursued by the organization more broadly and are often based on laws, regulations, policy and strategy guidance, and leadership priorities.

USEUCOM draws substantial sets of subordinate objectives, or sub-objectives, from guidance, strategy, and command plans. Figure 2.1, our framework for progress assessment, shows the association between guidance and subsequent planning in the

---

[1] Paul and Matthews, 2018.

Figure 2.1
Progress Assessment Framework

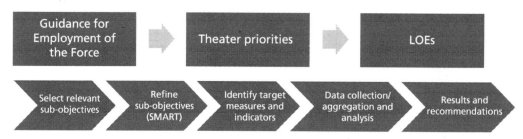

NOTE: Guidance for Employment of the Force is used primarily for planning and can inform theater priorities, which inform lines of effort (LOEs). Each LOE might have broad objectives or specific sub-objectives that should be considered when selecting relevant sub-objectives. At the time of this research, plans were underway to replace Guidance for Employment of the Force with the Global Force Management Allocation Plan and Global Force Management Implementation Guidance. SMART = specific, measurable, achievable, relevant, and time-bound.

top row.[2] The Guidance for Employment of the Force, which is informed by the Unified Command Plan and National Defense Strategy, is intended to guide the Joint Strategic Capabilities Plan. Combatant commanders can draw from the Joint Strategic Capabilities Plan when developing their theater priorities, theater campaign plans, and TCOs.[3] However, the Guidance for Employment of the Force and the Joint Strategic Capabilities Plan are used primarily for planning rather than as authoritative documents on strategic objectives. USEUCOM has several theater priorities with broad objectives that drive corresponding LOEs. Guidance from the combatant commander can inform which LOEs are to be given priority over others at any given time. A particular LOE might have multiple sub-objectives, including intermediate military objectives, that might be addressed by a range of OAIs.

Selecting Relevant Sub-Objectives

After identifying relevant priorities, goals, or objectives toward which progress will be assessed, along with corresponding LOEs, ECJ39 will need to select relevant sub-objectives. This is a two-step process. In the first step, ECJ39 would identify and select candidate sub-objectives from theater priorities or corresponding LOEs. In the second step, it would engage with appropriate stakeholders and leadership to ensure

---

[2]   At the time of this research, DoD's Guidance for Employment of the Force was in place. However, the plan was to replace it with the Global Force Management Allocation Plan and Global Force Management Implementation Guidance.

[3]   Philip M. Breedlove, *United States European Command Theater Strategy*, Stuttgart, Germany; U.S. European Command, October 2015.

that the selected sub-objectives align with their needs. Soliciting input, feedback, and approval from stakeholders outside ECJ39, across relevant organizations, working groups, or staff sections, will help prevent gaps in understanding and in the subsequent assessment results. A clear process for selecting sub-objectives for ECJ39 progress assessments can also promote effective coordination among diverse stakeholders and ensure the relevance of the assessment results (see Figure 2.2).

To identify candidate sub-objectives within a single LOE, ECJ39 can first review the sub-objectives, including intermediate military objectives, associated with a particular theater priority in the latest USEUCOM TCO and then select those that are most relevant to ECJ39. This process should involve drafting a brief (one-to-three-sentence) summary explaining why each sub-objective was selected. Noting that a particular sub-objective is relevant to ECJ39 should not suggest that the sub-objective is relevant *only* to ECJ39. The sub-objectives and the justifications for their selection should be reviewed by the ECJ39 chief before they are shared with other stakeholders.

ECJ39 might want to determine the extent to which it has advanced toward meeting an LOE's objective by measuring that progress across the sub-objectives that are most applicable to ECJ39, specifically. This would suggest a need to understand progress toward an objective but not necessarily a requirement for detailed knowledge about the contributions of each individual effort. In this case, a progress assessment would be needed. Note that ECJ39 progress assessments would serve ECJ39 interests, but they could also provide information for other stakeholders. These stakeholders might include USEUCOM's J7, Exercises and Assessments, the directorate with primary responsibility for assessments and analyses of LOEs in the TCO. J7 collaborates with other staff sections, including ECJ39, to complete these assessments. Conversely, feedback from J7 and others can enhance understanding and increase the relevance of ECJ39 assessments.

After internal review by the ECJ39 chief, sub-objectives should be shared with and validated by both J7 and J3, operations. To assist these directorates also in their review, the documentation should include *all* sub-objectives under the theater priority in the TCO, highlighting the sub-objectives that have been selected and the justifi-

Figure 2.2
Selecting Relevant Sub-Objectives for Progress Assessment

ECJ39 identifies candidate sub-objectives.	ECJ39 engages with stakeholders for feedback and approval of sub-objectives.
• ECJ39 reviews sub-objectives and identifies those that are relevant to progress assessment.	• ECJ39 shares sub-objectives, including those identified as most relevant, with directorates. • ECJ39 incorporates directorate feedback and shares sub-objectives with working groups. • ECJ39 incorporates working group feedback and shares sub-objectives with ECJ39 chief.

cations for their selection. In addition to this list, ECJ39 should provide a clear and concise explanation for why it is undertaking the progress assessment, how feedback on the sub-objectives will be used, and how the final list of selected sub-objectives will be used by ECJ39 and could be used by other USEUCOM organizations. This explanation might include, for example, a description of how the feedback can help ensure alignment across ECJ39 or USEUCOM efforts and promote coordination and cooperation. To facilitate timely vetting of the sub-objectives, ECJ39 should also include a date by which feedback must be received from J7 and J3. After this date, ECJ39 can then incorporate component feedback, if any, and refine its sub-objective selections and associated justifications.

After modifying the list based on feedback from J7 and J3, ECJ39 should share it with appropriate working groups, including those responsible for elements of the theater priority associated with the sub-objectives (e.g., measurement-related working groups, effects development working groups, LOE working groups). Note that these working groups might change over time as groups are created, combined, or disbanded, so ECJ39 will need to seek out up-to-date information about active working groups that should address attributes of the progress assessment. In addition, feedback from working group members should be sought formally, as part of the working groups' activities.

Again, ECJ39 should provide these reviewers with a list of all sub-objectives under the theater priority in the TCO, highlighting the sub-objectives that have been selected and the justifications for their selection. The working groups should be provided with a similar clear and concise explanation for why ECJ39 is undertaking the progress assessment, how feedback on the sub-objectives will be used, and how the final list of selected sub-objectives will be used by ECJ39 and could be used by other USEUCOM organizations. Ideally, this documentation will be provided to each working group one to two weeks before its next scheduled meeting. At that meeting, working group members can discuss the list and ECJ39's decisions to include or exclude certain sub-objectives. After a working group meeting, members should be allowed at least one additional week to provide feedback. ECJ39 can then incorporate working group feedback, if any, and refine its sub-objective selections and associated justifications. The ECJ39 chief can adjudicate this process and should then review the list again, modifying it as needed. After obtaining the chief's approval, ECJ39 can advance to the next step in the progress assessment framework. This process should be reinitiated each time the TCO changes or as needed.

Refining Objectives

After selecting relevant sub-objectives and obtaining requisite approval of the selections, ECJ39 must then begin to refine the sub-objectives.[4] JP 5-0, *Joint Planning*, describes objectives as "clearly defined, decisive, and attainable goals toward which every operation is directed . . . that are specific, measurable, achievable, relevant, and time-bound," or *SMART*.[5] Ideally, all objectives and sub-objectives in the TCO, including intermediate military objectives, should be SMART, but if this is not the case for some of the selected sub-objectives, ECJ39 will need to make refinements to measure progress against them.

Refining the selected sub-objectives might require rearticulation, as shown in Figure 2.3. For example, the terms and concepts in each sub-objective might need to be defined and described in more detail, or there might be a need to specify additional supporting objectives or objectives that are subordinate to a broader objective. Addressing expansive and ambiguous objectives will require clarifying intent and performance targets. Therefore, changes would need to go through the process that generated the selected sub-objectives, presumably being reviewed by J5, strategy, plans, and policy directorate. Rather than formally clarifying and rearticulating the sub-objectives, an alternative is to maintain the wording of the current sub-objectives but write measures of effectiveness (MOEs) and MOE indicators (MOEIs). Decisions about when to pursue each of these options should be based on relationships and experience with the staff sections that hold primary responsibility for the associated objectives.

Ideally, ECJ39 would propose all requisite refinements to all selected sub-objectives, and relevant directorates and working groups would review these refinements, following the same general process used to select sub-objectives. However, this

Figure 2.3
Refining Selected Sub-Objectives for Progress Assessment

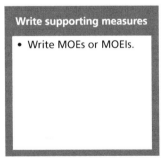

Rearticulate	Write supporting measures	Request feedback
• Describe terms and concepts in sub-objectives in more detail. • Specify additional supporting objectives or sub-objectives.	• Write MOEs or MOEIs.	• After initial refinement and specification, request feedback. – When requesting feedback, provide guidance on why it is needed and what is needed.

---

[4] Note that, formally, sub-objectives should be refined after they have been selected and approved by relevant stakeholders. In practice, initial refinement could occur in conjunction with the selection process, though it can be completed only after sub-objective selections are finalized.

[5] JP 5-0, *Joint Planning*, Washington, D.C.: U.S. Joint Chiefs of Staff, June 16, 2017, p. I-10.

might prove to be difficult. For example, without feedback, it might be difficult for ECJ39 to refine some of the selected sub-objectives, or time or resource constraints might hinder the collection of detailed feedback on all possible refinements.

To address this, ECJ39 may refine the sub-objectives—adding specificity, supporting objectives, or MOEs and MOEIs to all sub-objectives—and then request assistance from other directorates or organizations. It may be possible for working groups to provide assistance beyond simply reviewing and approving.

When requesting assistance from others, ECJ39 should clarify why feedback is needed and how it will be used. To reduce the burden on these entities, the request should highlight small sets of sub-objectives on which specific offices, components, or directorates should provide feedback. As before, for reference, the request should include all other sub-objectives already refined by ECJ39. It should also include a date by which feedback should be provided. After incorporating feedback from these entities, the list should be shared with relevant working groups, including working groups that address assessments and effects for relevant LOEs. After incorporating working group feedback, if any, the refined sub-objectives should be reviewed and approved by the ECJ39 chief, whose feedback should inform any additional modifications. ECJ39 should then submit the proposed revisions to J5/8, policy, strategy, partnering, and capabilities, for review and approval.

At this point in the process, ECJ39 has two lists: (1) a list of selected and approved sub-objectives that are relevant to ECJ39 and support the theater priorities and LOEs and (2) a list of SMART refined sub-objectives or supporting objectives that directly relate to the first list. If interaction with other staff sections through various working groups means that refinements reflected in the second list align with command-wide sub-objectives in the first list, that is a good thing.

Identifying Target Measures and Indicators

After receiving the requisite feedback and refining selected sub-objectives or developing supporting objectives, ECJ39 should identify target measures and indicators. This is a two-step process, as shown in Figure 2.4. The first step is to identify what information is needed to address questions regarding progress made, including, for example, identifying possible measures or proxy measures for SMART objectives or, if the alternative process for refining objectives was followed, identifying proxy measures for MOEs. In this step, the focus should be on determining what information and data might be needed, not on creating needs that might be addressed by currently collected data. In other words, the selected sub-objectives should drive the identification of measures and indicators, not the other way around. Attempts to collect and analyze data from a limited number of measures and indicators to assess progress toward multiple, wide-ranging sub-objectives can lead to the collection of data that are of limited use to

Figure 2.4
Process for Identifying Target Measures and Indicators

Identify what information is needed		Associate data sources and measures with sub-objectives
• Selected sub-objectives drive the identification of measures and indicators. • Consider whether currently collected measures might be used to address each sub-objective.		• Stakeholder feedback should guide additional data collection. • Prioritize measures. • Consider what data are available and what resources are needed for additional data collection.

offices, directorates, and units. This can also lead to knowledge gaps and create confusion. Resource and data collection limitations, as well as burdens on staff, will likely constrain which measures or indicators can be obtained, so stakeholder and leadership engagement when identifying measures or indicators is particularly worthwhile.

During the process of identifying target measures and indicators, ECJ39—in collaboration with a working group that addresses measures and indicators (e.g., an assessment working group)—should consider whether currently collected data might be used to address each sub-objective. This review of current measures or indicators should not be limited to those collected by ECJ39, specifically, but should also include those that other entities collect and are willing to share with ECJ39. These might include, for example, measures collected by USEUCOM components and organizations, the U.S. Department of State, embassies, and allies.

After the first step of identifying what information is needed, the second step is to associate relevant available data sources and measures with those information needs. Feedback from ECJ39 leadership and a working group that addresses measures and indicators should determine whether ECJ39 or others should pursue additional data collection to address the selected and refined sub-objectives. This will require making resource-constrained decisions about what to measure while considering the priority or importance of the measures. All critical indicators—such as those that most clearly address relevant progress—should be measured in some way. Note what data are already available and what resources are available for additional data collection, as well as which organization is responsible for collecting and analyzing that information. Currently collected data could be used to measure progress. Ideally, a measure or indicator of progress can be associated with each sub-objective. For a progress assessment, these measures or indicators might not provide detailed information about which OAIs are more or less influential in helping or hindering progress toward the selected sub-objectives or an overall objective. However, identified measures or indicators can provide a general indication of whether progress is occurring.

To promote clarity and understanding, this process for identifying target measures and indicators should end with a document outlining the data collection plan for progress assessment. For each measure or indicator, this plan would include (but should not be limited to) a description of the measure or indicator, data source, method of data collection, data owner, and frequency with which data are collected. Each measure should also be associated with its relevant sub-objective(s).

Collecting, Aggregating, and Analyzing Data

After identification, target measures and indicators should be defined and data should be collected (or aggregated, if the needed data are already available within the command) and analyzed. To assess progress, or change, one option is for analysts to examine changes observed among measures or indicators over time, also known as longitudinal data analysis or trend analysis.[6] This longitudinal analysis can begin with a baseline assessment, which provides information about a location or context before implementation of an OAI. If there is current, ongoing data collection addressing the location or context of interest, the collected data and results might be able to provide this initial information.

Data collection and analysis should be conducted by the organization (e.g., the USEUCOM office or directorate) that is responsible for collecting the relevant type of data. When to share information, what information to share, and how to provide this information should be determined through discussion and coordination among the office, directorate, or organization collecting the information; ECJ39; and the working group that addresses the measure or indicators. A data analysis plan, a "detailed document outlining procedures for conducting an analysis on data," helps foster mutual understanding of data and analyses.[7] The development of a data analysis plan might assist with coordination by providing guidance on how the data will be used and how to structure reports.

ECJ39 should hold primary responsibility for coordinating the receipt of relevant information at mutually acceptable time points, which should take into account the needs of the progress assessment and any potentially competing demands and activities among the organizations responsible for data collection and analysis.

---

[6]   Other options might draw from quasi-experimental research designs; see, for example, William R. Shadish, Thomas D. Cook, and Donald T. Campbell, *Experimental and Quasi-Experimental Designs for Generalized Causal Inference*, Boston, Mass.: Houghton Mifflin, 2001.

[7]   Kathleen Jablonski and Mark Guagliardo, *Data Analysis Plans: A Blueprint for Success Using SAS*, Cary, N.C.: SAS Institute, 2016.

Compiling and Sharing Results and Recommendations

Selecting relevant sub-objectives, incorporating input from stakeholders, refining the sub-objectives according to SMART principles, identifying target measures and indicators, collecting necessary data, and developing a data analysis plan should help ensure that the progress assessment will yield useful information. Results might be straightforward and could be generated by ECJ39 staff. Regardless, it is helpful to draft recommendations for interpreting and using the assessment information; these recommendations should also reflect lessons from the assessment process. For example, the results might reveal a need to review and modify approaches to achieving an objective or adjust the data collection and analysis. The content of the recommendations will vary, depending on the results of the data analysis. These recommendations might be developed by ECJ39 leadership and relevant working groups, including those that address measures and indicators, effects development, relevant LOEs, and joint effects. Each working group should review the results and draft or modify recommendations as needed. This feedback should inform subsequent actions and designs involving TCOs or plans.

Summary

This chapter described the primary and subsidiary steps involved in developing and implementing a progress assessment. Broadly, a progress assessment is a type of assessment, focused on one or more objectives, that measures movement toward objectives. Designing a progress assessment requires selecting relevant sub-objectives, refining selected sub-objectives, identifying target measures and indicators that address the selected sub-objectives, collecting and analyzing data, and clearly and concisely communicating results and recommendations.

CHAPTER THREE

A Framework for Developing and Implementing Performance and Effectiveness Assessments

When individuals or organizations need to understand overall advancement toward an objective, they may request or conduct a progress assessment (described in Chapter Two), which can incorporate measures from multiple OAIs. However, when they need a more thorough understanding of the functioning of one OAI or its contribution to overall progress, then a performance assessment in conjunction with an effectiveness assessment fits the bill. Performance assessments and effectiveness assessments are subordinate to progress assessments, and they can provide information that could be used in a broader progress assessment addressing the extent of overall advancement toward at least one objective.[1] A performance assessment provides feedback regarding the extent or quality of an OAI's implementation, and it includes measures of performance (MOPs).[2] An effectiveness assessment addresses contributions to advancement toward a goal or objective, and it includes MOEs and MOEIs.[3]

In this chapter, we build from our discussion of progress assessments to provide a framework to guide the development and implementation of both performance assessments and effectiveness assessments. As we did for progress assessments, we focus on applications to USEUCOM's ECJ39 and its interorganizational partners.

Broadly, this performance assessment and effectiveness assessment framework begins with the planning process and identifying OAIs of interest. Ideally, planning for assessment takes place at the same time as operational and activity planning.[4] Effectiveness assessment requires clearly articulated objectives, so those need to be either an input to the assessment planning process or refined as part of assessment planning.

---

[1] Paul and Matthews, 2018.

[2] JP 5-0 (2017) defines an MOP as "[a]n indicator used to measure a friendly action that is tied to measuring task accomplishment" (p. GL-12).

[3] JP 5-0 (2017) defines an MOE as "[a]n indicator used to measure a current system state, with change indicated by comparing multiple observations over time" (p. GL-12). It does not define *MOEI*, but JP 3-13 describes such indicators as "a unit, location, or event observed or measured, that can be used to assess an MOE. These are often used to add quantitative data points to qualitative MOEs and can assist an IO staff or IO cell in answering a question related to a qualitative MOE" (JP 3-13, 2014, p. IV-10).

[4] Paul et al., 2015.

(See the discussion in Chapter Two on refining objectives.) There will be a logic that connects an OAI with its intended purpose, but performance and effectiveness assessments require that this logic be explicitly spelled out as a theory of change.

A theory of change outlines how each OAI is intended to work, including details regarding necessary resources (inputs), outputs, and expected outcomes. A theory of change can involve many elements and connections. In part because of resource and time constraints, not all of these can or should be measured. Therefore, after developing or articulating a theory of change, assessment planners must identify which parts—elements or nodes—of the theory are already being measured and which need to be measured and how to measure those. At this point, data collection, aggregation, and analysis can occur. The results of this analysis can then be compiled to inform recommendations regarding a particular OAI. Throughout this process, it is important to solicit feedback and coordinate with relevant stakeholders across USEUCOM, including working groups and directorates. This step is critical to reducing misunderstandings, errors, and wasted time and resources. In this chapter, we expand on each of the steps in the framework, shown in Figure 3.1.

Figure 3.1
Performance Assessment and Effectiveness Assessment Framework

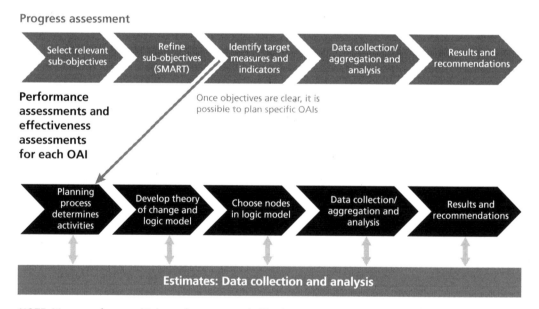

NOTE: Measures from multiple performance and effectiveness assessments across relevant OAIs can inform the broader progress assessment. Estimates can be used if necessary.

Developing SMART Objectives

Objectives provide the foundation for measuring progress, performance, and effectiveness. For example, to implement a progress assessment, an organization, including its stakeholders, must select relevant sub-objectives from guidance, such as a theater priority. After selection, the sub-objectives should be refined, as needed, to ensure that they are SMART. These refined sub-objectives inform the identification of target measures and indicators for a broader progress assessment, as discussed in Chapter Two. They should also inform the development and implementation of individual OAIs, which can be monitored and evaluated through more-specific performance and effectiveness assessments. A named operation or exercise, a distinct effort to influence or persuade a group or population (e.g., a locally targeted multimedia campaign), or regular dissemination of certain materials are all examples of distinct efforts that would each go through the performance assessment and effectiveness assessment framework.

Having and drawing from SMART sub-objectives, which might be developed during or as a result of a progress assessment, is a critical part of designing OAIs, as well as developing performance and effectiveness assessments. Attempts to create OAIs and use measures that address abstract, unobservable, impracticable, or irrelevant objectives that do not have a time horizon for completion can result in confusion, misused time, and wasted resources. Therefore, careful consideration should be given to objectives. Having SMART objectives will make it easier to plan, assess, and improve OAIs.

Planning for Assessment

Selected and refined sub-objectives should inform the joint operation planning process (JOPP) and other processes that determine a particular course of action (COA). In the components, examples include the Joint Operation Planning Process for Air (JOPPA), the Military Decision-Making Process (MDMP), and the Marine Corps planning process (MCPP). Figure 3.2 shows a high-level overview of steps in these planning processes.[5] After appropriate authorities recognize a need for military activities (planning initiation, receipt of mission), commanders and strategists must analyze the operational environment, drawing from selected and refined sub-objectives to determine its desired future state (mission analysis; problem framing). After that, possible COAs can be developed, analyzed, and compared against selected criteria (COA development,

---

[5]   Center for Army Lessons Learned, *MDMP: Lessons and Best Practices*, No. 15-06, March 2015; JP 3-30, *Joint Air Operations*, Washington, D.C.: U.S. Joint Chiefs of Staff, July 25, 2019; Headquarters, U.S. Department of the Army, *Psychological Operations Leaders Planning Guide*, Graphic Training Aid 33-01-001, November 2005; Curtis E. LeMay Center for Doctrine Development and Education, *The Joint Operation Planning Process for Air*, Maxwell Air Force Base, Ala., November 4, 2016.

Figure 3.2
Overview of a Possible Planning Process

analysis, and comparison). After commander approval, a detailed plan and orders can be developed and disseminated for the COA.

To better understand the current operational environment, planners might draw from a range of estimates. Estimates establish or help maintain situational awareness of a context, environment, or audience, and they can be developed by tracking trends, emerging concerns, developing opportunities, or changes related to a specific event.[6] Note that an objective is not required for estimates to be collected and analyzed. However, estimates can inform each step of the performance and effectiveness assessment framework, and that framework does require at least one sub-objective.

To contextualize the operational environment, planners might draw from estimates that they are already collecting, such as through traditional and digital or social media analyses. They can also request information about specific events or locations from the European Command Open Source Element, the components, or other staff directorates. After collecting and summarizing data to provide a clear and concise description of the relevant operational environment and its context, planners should share this information with relevant working groups, including those that address assessments and effects within relevant LOEs. Planners should ask members of these working groups to review the collected information and to provide feedback by a specified date. Planners should incorporate this feedback into their description of the operational environment or collaborate with working group members to address discrepancies.

Once the operational context and problems have been framed, COAs can be developed and analyzed. ECJ39 can begin this process by outlining a potential COA that addresses selected and refined sub-objectives. After development, this outline should be coordinated with the USEUCOM J7 and J3 directorates. To ensure timely feedback, ECJ39 should also include a date by which J7 and J3 feedback regarding the approach and plan must be received. After using this feedback to modify the COA, ECJ39 should share the COA outline with appropriate working groups for analysis, including groups that might have responsibility for elements of the theater priority of focus (e.g., effects development working groups, LOE working groups).

---

6   Paul and Matthews, 2018.

Although SMART objectives should have been an input to the planning process (or emerged as part of that process), in practice, OAIs are sometimes planned in the absence of a clear connection to SMART objectives. Should this occur, it is incumbent on assessment planners to refine objectives to satisfy SMART criteria before proceeding with assessment planning.

Developing (or Modifying) a Theory of Change and Logic Model

After planning processes to determine COAs, ECJ39 should develop a theory of change for each OAI (see Figure 3.3). If an existing theory of change exists for a similar effort, ECJ39 could draw from and tailor it to the new effort. A theory of change describes the connections among specified resources, activities, contextual factors, and outcomes. It identifies how the planned elements of an effort will achieve specified objectives.[7] In doing so, a theory of change promotes examination of underlying assumptions regarding elements of a particular effort and links between them, making implicit hypotheses and beliefs explicit.

A logic model is a visualization tool that can assist with developing a theory of change. A logic model is a visual diagram that shows the connections among various elements of an OAI. Note that the approach to specifying the end state to be achieved (ends), actions to achieve that end state (ways), and resources required to take those actions (means) is a common military process and similar to articulating a theory of change.[8] In Chapter Four, we provide additional information about logic models and an example of how they might be used.

Briefly, to develop a theory of change, an organization must consider the inputs, or resources, required to implement and sustain an OAI.[9] These inputs could include the funding, number of personnel, and type of expertise required to implement the

Figure 3.3
Process for Developing a Theory of Change and Corresponding Logic Model

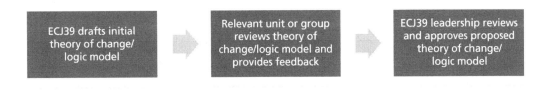

---

[7]   Paul et al., 2015.

[8]   Christopher Paul, *Assessing and Evaluating Department of Defense Efforts to Inform, Influence, and Persuade: Worked Example*, Santa Monica, Calif.: RAND Corporation, RR-809/4-OSD, 2017.

[9]   For an in-depth description of the process for developing a theory of change, see Paul et al., 2015.

OAI. Activities (i.e., verbs connected to resource use) and the outputs from those activities must also be considered and incorporated into the theory of change. Outputs can be measured using performance assessments. Outputs contribute to outcomes, or effects, which can be measured using effectiveness assessments. Outcomes are longer-term impacts. A logic model shows each of these elements and the connections among them.

Although one individual or organization can draft an initial theory of change for an OAI, more than one will need to review the logic and provide input to identify constraints, barriers, disrupters, and unintended consequences that need to be addressed in the theory.[10] ECJ39 can draft an initial theory of change. However, a relevant unit or group, such as an effects working group, will need to review the theory or its corresponding logic model and provide feedback on the assumptions made within it. Relevant units or groups include those that are responsible for the sub-objective being addressed or aspects of the theory of change being developed, such as effects measurement. In requesting review of a draft theory of change, ECJ39 should provide the unit or group with clear evaluation guidance. This might include, for example, guidance to consider whether elements are missing (e.g., missing resources), whether elements are labeled appropriately (e.g., properly identified as resources, activities, outputs, or outcomes), and whether connections among elements are correct. In-person discussions with group members might assist in rapidly articulating and refining the theory. After working group feedback has been incorporated, ECJ39 leadership should review, and, if no immediate changes are needed, approve the theory of change. After OAI implementation, flaws in the model might be discovered, so subsequent modifications and corrections may be required. These changes should be discussed by working group members and briefed to ECJ39 leadership.

Choosing What to Measure

After developing a theory of change and logic model, it is necessary to determine which nodes in the logic model to measure (see Figure 3.4). It will likely not be possible to measure all of the elements and connections in the model; fortunately, it is not always necessary to measure everything. As we discussed in previous research and worked examples, not all elements address fundamental assumptions or uncertainties, and attempting to measure everything can be costly in terms of time, personnel, and money.[11] The logic model can assist in identifying candidate measures that address core components of an OAI, vulnerable assumptions, and critical uncertainties. Priority should be given to measuring parts of the logic model that address core cause-and-

---

[10] Paul, 2017.

[11] Paul, 2017.

Figure 3.4
Process for Choosing Nodes to Measure

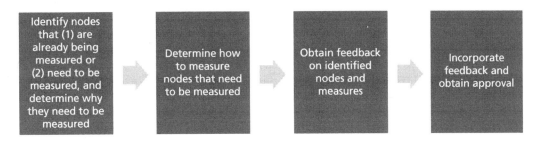

effect relationships among elements of the OAI and uncertain assumptions, as well as to identifying successes and failures, rather than simply addressing indicators of success. Core relationships and elements are those that are required to achieve intended effects. Planners should also consider whether there are nodes for which currently collected data are available or on which data can easily be obtained. If there are nodes for which data are not currently being collected but for which data collection would prove useful, ECJ39 should identify these nodes and relevant measures and then request assistance and resources accordingly. In other words, selecting and prioritizing nodes requires addressing what needs to be measured, what is already being measured, and what is not already being measured but needs to be.

Choosing elements of a theory of change requires identifying which elements are already being addressed with current measures and which elements need to be measured. Then, it is necessary to determine how to measure the latter and whether potentially relevant indicators (including estimates) are already being collected and by whom. ECJ39 can begin this process by identifying elements within the logic model that have or need measures, describing why a certain element needs to be measured (e.g., What makes it a key component of the theory of change?), and proposing how to measure elements for which measures are not already available. It might not be feasible to develop direct measures for every element, in which case proxy measures might be necessary. And when measure reliability is potentially low, it could be worthwhile to use several measures to address a single key element in the logic model.

After measures that are or could be collected have been identified, this information should be shared with appropriate working groups (e.g., effects development working groups, LOE working groups). In sharing this information, ECJ39 should request feedback regarding whether all relevant measures on its list can be used in the model. In addition, ECJ39 should request input regarding how to measure elements for which there are no or very few currently collected measures; this feedback can help inform subsequent requests for assistance and resources. Specifying a date by which feedback will be needed should ensure timely turnaround.

After feedback has been incorporated, the ECJ39 chief should review the identified elements and measures, providing final approval after any issues or questions have been addressed. When no or few current measures are available to address certain elements, ECJ39 will need to identify organizations that can collect those measures and determine the amount of funding that will be needed to do so.

Collecting, Aggregating, and Analyzing Data

The next step of the process is data collection, analysis, and aggregation. Measures identified in the previous step can be used to evaluate changes over time. However, this often requires a baseline measurement of the conditions or context of interest. Currently collected estimates, identified in the previous step, might provide baselines before program or effort implementation. Because effects can take time to materialize, monitoring might focus on performance assessments during initial OAI implementation. Later in the process, effectiveness assessments can provide feedback regarding outcomes.

A data analysis plan can assist with data collection and analysis. Specifically, this plan would outline who will collect and process the data and how the data will be analyzed, as well as approximate time points for reporting the results of specified measures. By developing this plan, ECJ39 can reduce the potential for confusion regarding how to analyze and interpret data once they have been collected.

Compiling and Sharing Results and Recommendations

ECJ39 should closely monitor collected data to evaluate key assumptions quickly and identify barriers or disrupters as early as possible. If the results show that assumptions in the logic model are flawed or incorrect, they will need to be modified or replaced, and corresponding changes will need to be made to the OAI's execution and measurement plan. Likewise, if the results reveal barriers or disrupters, then ECJ39 will need to determine how to overcome them.

ECJ39 should provide regular, brief updates to interested stakeholders, describing the results derived from the collected data. These stakeholders might include effects development and LOE working groups. The updates should incorporate clear and concise summaries of results and explicitly capture the relevance of the results for the OAI of interest. The frequency with which these updates are provided and to whom can be determined through discussion and coordination with stakeholders.

When flawed assumptions, barriers, or disrupters are identified, they should be highlighted in the updates to stakeholders, alongside recommendations and planned actions for addressing them. ECJ39 should request feedback from stakeholders on proposed changes or actions and specify a date by which this feedback will be needed. Once the stakeholder feedback is incorporated, any resulting changes to the logic model and planned actions for addressing barriers or disrupters should be reviewed and approved by the ECJ39 chief.

Summary

This chapter described the steps involved in developing and implementing performance and effectiveness assessments. A performance assessment addresses the extent or quality of implementation of a particular OAI, and an effectiveness assessment addresses the extent to which an OAI contributes to advancement toward a goal. The performance and effectiveness assessment framework presented in this chapter draws on SMART objectives to inform the activity planning process. Then, planners must develop or modify a theory of change/logic model and choose which nodes to measure. After that, data can be collected and analyzed, and results and recommendations can be communicated to appropriate stakeholders.

CHAPTER FOUR

Demonstration Application: Addressing the Effects of Major Coalition Exercises

As noted earlier in this report, one key input that each commander requires to make dynamic military decisions is information on the effect(s) of past and ongoing OAIs. Information on the effects of past efforts helps commanders identify those that could make the greatest contribution to campaign goals while promoting awareness of those that appear ineffective or in need of reform. Often, the best approach is unknown, but information on the effectiveness of an effort can be vital for commanders to know, as early as possible, whether unproven techniques appear to be working well.

In any form, information on the effectiveness of an OAI is derived through a continuous process of systematic data collection and analysis (see Chapter Three for more on performance assessments).[1] Although the criticality of this information to commander decisions is widely acknowledged, and there are existing frameworks to guide DoD personnel through this process,[2] many planners struggle to design performance assessments and effectiveness assessments that meet commanders' decision needs.

The previous chapters provided an overview of assessment frameworks that draw from military doctrine. However, discussions with ECJ39 planners suggested a gap between the principles espoused in assessment doctrine and the real-world practical application of those principles. ECJ39 planners require more-vivid examples illustrating how to approach the difficult problems that they face. Prior RAND research on assessing efforts to inform, influence, and persuade discussed the difficulties facing assessment practitioners who focus on the IE,[3] and this chapter seeks to help ECJ39 planners overcome these common challenges.[4]

---

[1] JP 3-0, 2017.

[2] See, for example, JP 3-13, 2014.

[3] Paul et al., 2015.

[4] We provided ECJ39 with examples specific to USEUCOM operational needs as part of this project.

Context and Challenges

Performance and effectiveness assessments provide information that helps commanders formulate strategies with the best chances of achieving objectives and learn over time. Information on the execution and effects of past and ongoing OAIs provides a necessary feedback loop to commanders so that they can learn from and adjust efforts that are struggling and reinforce those that are succeeding. For this reason, the Joint Concept for Operating in the Information Environment sets a high bar for operational effectiveness assessment by calling for a "required capability" to "identify, optimize, and assess the effectiveness of the full range of options that integrate physical and informational power to produce desired psychological effects."[5]

Although the value of such a capability is clear, ECJ39 planners face multiple challenges in attempting to design performance and effectiveness assessments for USEUCOM efforts, particularly in the case of resource-intensive military exercises involving one or more partner nations. First, these exercises are often large and complex, demanding interoperability across multiple capabilities and partner forces. Discerning the contribution of such activities to various objectives (including foreign policy objectives) is inherently difficult. A second difficulty is that USEUCOM exercises might intend to affect adversaries' future decisions by shaping their perceptions—planning for which is fraught with imperfect knowledge and measurement limitations. Deterring adversaries from unwanted behaviors, for example, requires careful inputs to adversaries' perceptions and calculations that make them view alternative behaviors as more attractive than the behaviors that the exercise is trying to deter.[6] The complexity of adversary motivations regarding aggression, the difficulty of observing shifts in such motivations over time, and the potential influence of external factors place limits on the capabilities of effectiveness assessments.[7] Finally, the behaviors that exercises seek to affect, such as partner investments in capabilities and deterrence of adversaries, involve infrequent events, making it difficult to confidently identify causal links between a particular effort and the resulting actions. In terms of deterrence, for example, it is likely impossible to definitively link a particular USEUCOM exercise to an adversary's decision to act aggressively or show restraint.

In the end, commanders must weigh COAs based on some criteria (formal or informal) for what will be most effective. The challenge facing USEUCOM planners, then, is to continuously refine different assessment structures so that they incrementally improve the quality of information provided to commanders. This chapter rec-

---

[5]   DoD, *Joint Concept for Operating in the Information Environment (JCOIE)*, Washington, D.C., July 25, 2018, p. xi, Table 1.

[6]   Michael J. Mazarr, *Understanding Deterrence*, Santa Monica, Calif.: RAND Corporation, PE-295-RC, 2018.

[7]   John Gale, Stephenie Loux, and Andrew Coburn, *Creating Program Logic Models: A Toolkit for State Flex Programs*, Minneapolis, Minn., Chapel Hill, N.C., and Portland, Me.: Flex Monitoring Team, University of Minnesota, University of North Carolina, and University of Southern Maine, April 2006.

ommends some first steps for improving the quality of performance and effectiveness assessments in the case of large coalition exercises that are typical in USEUCOM and elsewhere. The principles that we discuss in this context could also help inform assessments of other OAIs that face similar challenges.

Refining Objectives by Enumerating Critical Pieces of Information

As discussed in Chapters Two and Three, JP 5-0 defines *objectives* as "clearly defined, decisive, and attainable goals toward which every operation is directed" and explicitly calls for objectives to be SMART.[8] In practice, ECJ39 planners often inherit high-level objectives that lack the SMART attributes, making the objectives impossible to assess as written. The first way that ECJ39 planners can improve the design of different types of assessments, even in a challenging environment, is to work toward refining objectives.

To anchor the discussion, consider two overarching goals that are common in a coalition environment: strengthening partnerships and deterring adversaries. For example, in 2018, NATO Secretary General Jens Stoltenberg stated that an upcoming major security cooperation exercise "sends a clear message, to our nations and to any potential adversary: NATO does not seek confrontation, but we stand ready to defend all Allies against any threat."[9] This statement implies information-related objectives involving both partner nations and potential adversaries. But these objectives would need additional refinement (i.e., the application of SMART principles) before ECJ39 planners could assess the contribution of the exercise to information-related objectives. The following are a subset of critical pieces of information that are often needed to refine objectives.

Specify the Target Audience for Each Message

As in the NATO exercise example, it is common for senior leaders to speak of "messages" sent to partner or adversary nations. This level of generality is a problem for ECJ39 planners, because more specificity in terms of the target audience—the individuals or groups that an OAI seeks to influence—is required to determine whether the right message was sent and whether it was influential in the way that senior leaders intended.[10] Objectives tend to be overly general when a given OAI is intended to influence many target audiences, in which case ECJ39 planners can formulate subobjectives for each audience to ensure that the assessment plan is postured to measure

---

[8] JP 5-0, 2017.

[9] NATO, "NATO Secretary General Briefs on Exercise Trident Juncture," October 24, 2018.

[10] See Paul and Matthews, 2018.

all relevant effects. Table 4.1 provides some examples of possible target audiences for a set of hypothetical IE-related objectives.

Specify the Desired Behaviors of Partners and Adversaries

Another way in which objectives could be refined is by specifying partner and adversary behaviors that an OAI seeks to promote or deter. Often, ECJ39 planners inherit information-related objectives that focus solely on influencing partner or adversary attitudes, beliefs, or intentions, which are useful insofar as changes in these predispositions lead to changes in behaviors. For example, a program or effort that successfully shifts attitudes (generally, favorable or unfavorable feelings)[11] might drive behaviors that contribute to a desired end state or objective. However, if planners know the behaviors that they want the program or effort to drive, they should specify those behaviors directly in the objectives.[12] In addition to enabling better assessment design, articulating specific desired behaviors will likely improve other parts of the planning process, such as mission analysis and COA development.[13]

To continue the earlier example, if an exercise is intended to influence adversaries in a way that contributes to deterrence, then articulating the particular adversary behaviors that the exercise is seeking to deter will help ECJ39 craft measurement plans and follow-on efforts that amplify the message of the exercise. This clarity is essential because the optimal deterrent message likely differs for different behaviors, a topic we discuss in the section "Example Theory of Change for Deterrence," later in this chapter.

Table 4.1
Sample Target Audiences for Hypothetical Information-Related Objectives

If the objective of the OAI is to . . .	The target audience might be . . .
Demonstrate commitment to **partner governments**	Partner-nation political and military senior leaders
Increase **partner-nation public support** for a partnership with the United States	Segments of the civilian population that do not already support a partnership with the United States
Deter **adversaries** or deescalate tension	Adversary nation political and military senior leaders
Shape beliefs about U.S. intentions among **populations of adversary countries**	Segments of the adversary civilian population whose influence would contribute to broader goals

---

[11] Martin Fishbein and Icek Ajzen, *Belief, Attitude, Intention, and Behavior: An Introduction to Theory and Research*, Reading, Mass.: Addison-Wesley, 1975.

[12] Paul et al., 2015.

[13] JP 5-0, 2017.

Be Explicit About the Time Horizon

Part of the difficulty in assessing exercises with partner nations stems from the fact that the time horizon for change often extends far beyond the immediate aftermath of a single exercise. Major efforts to show resolve might take several iterations before adversary perceptions begin to shift. Even if there is great uncertainty in the timeline, however, leaving the objective completely open-ended could invite errors by causing commanders to either judge an effort too soon or continue it indefinitely with no discernable progress. Writing objectives that are time-bound—that is, clarifying intended time horizons for objectives that are published in guidance—permits the best use of limited resources. Measurement efforts can be synchronized with the time horizon of the expected change or the relevant decision cycle.[14]

Developing and Articulating a Theory of Change or Logic Model

Once ECJ39 planners have refined their objectives, most often by seeking additional clarity on key pieces of information, the next step for designing a comprehensive performance or effectiveness assessment is to fully enumerate a theory of change, which is defined as "the clear, logical connections between an OAI and desired outcome, including intermediate steps between the current situation and desired outcome."[15] The theory of change is a critical step in assessment design; simply articulating the intended logic behind an OAI often invites immediate refinement when too much generality hides assumptions that are unlikely to hold. Furthermore, a proper logic model that highlights the connection between a particular effort and its objectives will suggest areas to measure. If the effort is not successful, the logic model will help planners and assessment practitioners identify the point in the causal chain where the failure occurred.

As noted in Chapter Three, logic models typically include the following elements,[16] forming a causal chain that maps the full theory of change—from required inputs to desired impact (Figure 4.1):

- *inputs:* resources required to execute an OAI.
- *activities:* the actual undertakings of the OAI, or the actions necessary to translate inputs into outputs.

---

[14] Paul et al., 2015, offers the following helpful advice for developing time-bound objectives: "Time boundaries need not be more precise than the science will allow, and they can be phrased as opportunities to assess progress and revisit plans rather than times after which progress will be considered to be lagging" (p. 27).

[15] Paul and Matthews, 2018, p. 3. Also see Chapter Three, in which we discuss theories of change in the context of developing performance and effectiveness assessments.

[16] See Paul et al., 2015, for more details.

Figure 4.1
Basic Theory of Change/Logic Model Template

- *outputs:* things that are produced by conducting the activities, including traditional MOPs and indicators that activities were executed as planned.
- *outcomes:* the result or consequence of an OAI's implementation, such as the expected change in the target population.
- *impact:* the expected, cumulative, long-term, or enduring contribution, likely to a larger campaign or superordinate goal.

Example Theory of Change for Strengthening Partnership

Considering the case of the security cooperation exercise, let us suppose, for illustrative purposes, that one objective is to increase civilian population beliefs in U.S. resolve to defend the partner nation, because planning assumptions stipulate that this will make the partnership more resilient. Establishing a theory of change forces USEUCOM planners to specify each step in the causal process linking the planned components of the exercise to the refined strategic objective. A theory of change might be articulated as follows:

> Resources and access will be provided to a robust information campaign to publicize the successful partner exercise. ECJ39 analysts have identified a key target audience of civilians within the partner nation whose level of support is lower than desired and is amenable to bolstering. Synchronized communication efforts will produce a slate of daily products and release them over mediums thought to reach the target audience. The target audience will receive the message, comprehend it, and interpret the exercise-related information as evidence of U.S. commitment and resolve to defending the partner nation, thereby increasing the target audience's belief that the United States will defend it in a crisis.

The example theory of change highlights many links in the causal chain between an OAI (in this case, an information campaign) and the objective (bolstering confidence among partner-nation civilians). The theory of change highlights inputs that are needed (e.g., access, analysis of target audience attitudes), particular activities, outputs (products produced), and outcomes (exposure, beliefs). With these links explicitly stated, it becomes clearer where measurement efforts should be directed to assess the success of each portion of the effort and the validity of the assumptions that string together the theory of change. We discuss measurement efforts in more detail in the section "Choosing What to Measure by Developing a Detailed Measurement Plan," later in this chapter.

Example Theory of Change for Deterrence

Among the most daunting tasks facing ECJ39 planners is attempting to understand how coalition exercises could contribute to deterrence. Formulating a deterrence strategy is uniquely difficult because effectiveness requires an accurate understanding of adversary decision processes and relevant criteria. Building a theory of change that leads to increased deterrence starts with clarifying an official theory of deterrence or a set of deterrence assumptions under which to formulate a given OAI (and subsequent assessments of that effort).

One possibility is the model described in the Deterrence Operations Joint Operating Concept (DO JOC), which states that "deterrence operations convince adversaries not to take actions that threaten US vital interests . . . by credibly threatening to deny benefits and/or impose costs, while encouraging restraint by convincing the actor that restraint will result in an acceptable outcome."[17] A few points from the DO JOC and other deterrence scholarship are worth highlighting:

- The DO JOC delineates that OAIs can contribute to deterrence by affecting the benefits and costs of an action (from the adversary's perspective), as well as the consequences if the adversary takes no action.
- The DO JOC highlights credibility as an additional factor. A given OAI can enhance the credibility of a deterrence message by demonstrating the will and capability to respond.[18] Both will and capability could be relevant to security cooperation exercises.
- Clarity about the actions or behaviors that USEUCOM seeks to deter is vital to effectiveness in two ways. A fundamental condition of successful deterrence is that the adversary knows what the United States and partner nations seek to deter and what the coalition response will be if deterrence fails.[19]

Internally to ECJ39, this same clarity is required to properly nest individual OAIs into the official deterrence theory by linking them to the adversary's cost-benefit calculus. For example, when one side has a credible military advantage (sufficient to deter a large-scale attack), adversaries might respond with calculated uses of limited force that are much more difficult to deter.[20] If ECJ39 planners are formulating an effectiveness

---

[17] DoD, *Deterrence Operations Joint Operating Concept, Version 2.0*, Washington, D.C., December 2006, p. 3.

[18] Mazarr, 2018.

[19] Mazarr, 2018.

[20] Paul K. Huth, "Deterrence and International Conflict: Empirical Findings and Theoretical Debates," *Annual Review of Political Science*, Vol. 2, June 1999.

assessment of an effort designed to contribute to deterrence through specific, small-scale behavior changes, they need to consider the costs and benefits to the adversary, as well as the credibility of U.S. responses regarding these behaviors.

A theory of change for deterrence in our example, then, should begin with the link between the components of the exercise and the relevant costs and benefits that the adversary associates with targeted undesirable actions. For example, suppose one of the objectives of the exercise is to contribute to deterring adversary senior leaders from ordering a foreign military incursion below the threshold for conflict that undermines partner-nation sovereignty. A theory of change linking a component of the exercise to this objective could be articulated as follows:

> Consistent investments and security cooperation efforts have resulted in intelligence, surveillance, and reconnaissance (ISR) capabilities that make the partner nation more likely to detect and respond to adversary actions. Exercise planners have orchestrated a demonstration of these capabilities that will feature prominently in the exercise, which will be shown directly to adversary observers of the exercise and indirectly to adversary leaders via adversary ISR collection. Adversary senior leaders will conclude that these capabilities increase the risk of incursion failure, decreasing the probability that they will reap the benefits of ordering an incursion and thereby increasing the likelihood of deterrence.

With this theory of change, it is more apparent that not all links in the causal chain will be directly measurable.

Choosing What to Measure by Developing a Detailed Measurement Plan

Articulating a fully formed theory of change/logic model that specifies (at a minimum) the required inputs, activities, outputs, and outcomes that undergird an OAI and the desired effect on the target population contributes directly to a strategic measurement approach. Using the logic model as a guide will help ECJ39 planners ensure that the best available measures are in place at each step. Good measures are valid, reliable, feasible, and useful, and ECJ39 planners can use a blend of quantitative and qualitative techniques to collect information.[21]

Data quality usually comes at a price, so designing a measurement plan necessarily involves discerning the cause-and-effect relationships in the logic model that require high-quality measures from those for which cheaper measures with weaker attributes

---

[21] According to Paul et al., 2015, *validity* refers to the correspondence between the measure and the construct. *Reliability* is the degree of consistency in measurement. *Feasibility* is the extent to which data can be generated with a reasonable level of effort, and *usefulness* captures whether the measure is meaningful to end users and stakeholders.

will do. The importance that ECJ39 planners place on measuring something should be based on two factors: the uncertainty in the relationship and the cost of being wrong. Critical steps in the logic model that are highly theoretical or unproven will require high-quality measures so that firm conclusions can be drawn for future programs or efforts.

In our first example, in which an information campaign seeks to influence the beliefs of a partner-nation civilian population, each step should be amenable to some sort of measurement. A sensible measurement plan might collect information on the most important inputs and traditional MOPs that capture the production and dissemination of media products, coupled with data collection that probes the characteristics of the target audience (e.g., through focus groups or surveys), its exposure and comprehension, and the relationship between these factors and beliefs about U.S. commitment. Content analysis of the media environment could also contribute to an understanding of whether the desired message was communicated and received as intended. Media content could contain information about the baseline sentiments of the target audience (i.e., attitudes prior to the exercise), the dissemination of the desired message or themes, and reactions to the message, but ECJ39 assessment practitioners should pay careful attention to whether the media content is representative of the target audience.[22] By analyzing and synthesizing all available information from these sources, the full assessment could provide a clearer picture to commanders of whether required inputs were in place, whether the components of the effort were executed as planned, whether the target audience received the message, and the degree to which the audience's self-reported beliefs were affected.[23]

In our second example theory of change, in which an exercise demonstrates a new capability that is intended to increase deterrence, it is more difficult to populate the logic model with ideal measures. Although the inputs to the exercise and the demonstration of capabilities are measurable, whether and how the demonstration affects adversary decisions will remain veiled. Public statements made by adversary leaders might be strategic or deceptive, and media coverage is unlikely to be a good proxy for senior decisionmaker views. In this case, the best information on adversary leaders' interpretation of the exercise will likely come from intelligence analysis of future behaviors, and ECJ39 should work with personnel in ECJ2 to identify possible indicators, collections, and analyses that could support these important but challenging assessments. The DO JOC recommends that effectiveness assessments measure adversary responses to deterrent actions, as well as "expected and unexpected 2nd and 3rd order impacts."[24] Perhaps adversary force posture, tactics and training, or military

---

[22] Paul et al., 2015.

[23] A further refinement might specify in the theory of change observable behaviors that should result from a belief in U.S. commitment and then measure those behaviors.

[24] DoD, 2006, p. 53.

investments would change if the capability demonstrated was significant enough, and such changes might be partially observable. Beyond adversary leaders' views of the capabilities demonstrated, the final link to the impact relative to deterrence is never directly observable. Even if deterrence ultimately fails, that would not necessarily mean that the capability demonstration did not have the intended effect. For this link, the best COA is to rely on clear logic and a sound theory of deterrence, which can be informed by research on adversary worldviews and experimentation (i.e., wargames).[25] Conducting formative research to understand how adversaries will interpret a particular effort could be resource-intensive. Still, such costs could be justified based on the uncertainty surrounding adversary thinking and the fact that significant errors in the assumed logic of deterrence efforts could render the effort ineffective (or worse, could have the opposite effect and cause adversaries to become more aggressive).

Even in such cases as deterrence, when the changes in perceptions that an effort seeks to affect are not necessarily directly measurable, grounding measurement plans in an explicit theory of change represented in a logic model can still provide important feedback to commanders. For example, this approach can help commanders distinguish between *program failure* and *theory failure*.[26] Figure 4.2 illustrates this concept with a simplistic representation of a logic model for our deterrence example. In the top row, the intended capability demonstration was successful, and the official deterrence theory was correct, so the results are the desired outcomes and impact. The middle row represents a case of theory failure, in which metrics indicate that inputs were in place, the demonstration was executed as intended, and the output of interest—the rapid response time enabled by the new ISR capability—is in view of the adversary. However, in this example, the theory about the increased response time being a decisive factor in adversary decisions is flawed, as indicated by the main outcome (a change to some dimension of the adversary's force posture). *This information is useful to commanders*, who now know that the theory of deterrence is incomplete and in need of revision. On the other hand, the bottom row presents a case in which input and output metrics indicate that the capability increase was not actually demonstrated. In this case, performance assessment will help the commander avoid the errant conclusion that the capabilities did not deter the adversary, informing decisions about whether to allocate additional resources for a more successful demonstration of the capability.

---

[25] According to the DO JOC, experimentation serves to "exercise and improve the concept; develop and refine deterrence scenarios; vet deterrence assessments; help determine and measure 2nd and 3rd order effects (including interactions across actors and regions); and help characterize and manage uncertainty" (DoD, 2006, p. 54).

[26] Paul, Yeats et al., 2015.

Figure 4.2
Program Failure Versus Theory Failure in Performance and Effectiveness Assessment of Deterrence-Related Activities

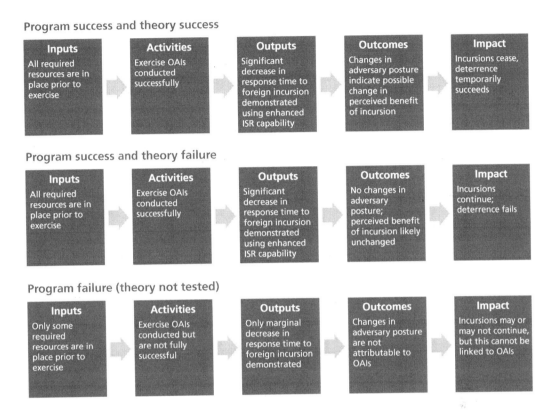

Program success and theory success

Inputs	Activities	Outputs	Outcomes	Impact
All required resources are in place prior to exercise	Exercise OAIs conducted successfully	Significant decrease in response time to foreign incursion demonstrated using enhanced ISR capability	Changes in adversary posture indicate possible change in perceived benefit of incursion	Incursions cease, deterrence temporarily succeeds

Program success and theory failure

Inputs	Activities	Outputs	Outcomes	Impact
All required resources are in place prior to exercise	Exercise OAIs conducted successfully	Significant decrease in response time to foreign incursion demonstrated using enhanced ISR capability	No changes in adversary posture; perceived benefit of incursion likely unchanged	Incursions continue; deterrence fails

Program failure (theory not tested)

Inputs	Activities	Outputs	Outcomes	Impact
Only some required resources are in place prior to exercise	Exercise OAIs conducted but are not fully successful	Only marginal decrease in response time to foreign incursion demonstrated	Changes in adversary posture are not attributable to OAIs	Incursions may or may not continue, but this cannot be linked to OAIs

Summary

This chapter applied steps from the previously described performance assessment and effectiveness assessment framework to military exercises. Making progress toward strategic objectives requires accurate information about the effectiveness of past OAIs. However, the scale and complexity of strategic influence efforts, such as exercises, can make it difficult to apply the doctrinal assessment design template. Real-world practice often involves many information gaps and measurement difficulties. Still, it is possible to facilitate incremental improvements in the quality of performance and effectiveness assessment information that commanders receive—if those who design the assessments refine the objectives and further vet the theory of change behind the efforts, and if measurement plans focus on all nodes in the chain of causality between a given OAI and its objectives (to the extent that this is possible). Furthermore, adding specificity invites refinement, so even imperfect effectiveness assessments can contribute to better strategy over time as organizations learn from past efforts and regularly refine theories on the determinants of friendly or adversary actions. By contrast, the alternative of being vague when there are information gaps invites error and could cause organizations to repeat past mistakes.

CHAPTER FIVE

Conclusions and Recommendations

Designing, implementing, and effectively using assessments of efforts to inform, influence, and persuade requires that planners understand and manage multiple difficult challenges. These include addressing how to accurately measure cognitive dimensions, disentangling the effects of various factors on the dimensions of interest (whether cognitive or behavioral), determining how to meaningfully aggregate information to determine overall progress toward an objective, and consistently measuring the efforts over time. Frameworks for assessment design can assist planners by ensuring that they consider how results might be used, which attributes of assessment design are important, and who should provide feedback regarding the design and use of assessments.

When planners need to obtain information about overall progress toward an objective or set of objectives, they can design and implement a progress assessment. A progress assessment is not limited to addressing one program or effort. Rather, it can include multiple OAIs, provided they are all intended to address the same objectives.[1] In the context of DoD, campaign assessments and operations assessments can be considered types of progress assessments. Important first steps in the design and implementation of a progress assessment include identifying the critical objectives toward which progress will be assessed and refining selected objectives so that they are SMART. Selecting, refining, and clearly communicating well-defined objectives can help ensure that relevant stakeholders have a common understanding of what a progress assessment is, or should be, measuring. Importantly, these objectives require thoughtful review and feedback from stakeholders. After objectives have been selected and refined, the next steps of a progress assessment can be pursued, including identifying target measures, collecting and analyzing data, and communicating results and recommendations.

Ensuring the advancement of multiple OAIs toward one or more objectives is not the only possible reason to collect, analyze, and communicate the results of various measures. Another purpose for doing so is to gain a more thorough understanding of the functioning of an individual OAI. Performance assessments and effectiveness

---

[1] Paul and Matthews, 2018.

assessments can support this understanding. These types of assessments are subordinate to progress assessments. A performance assessment includes MOPs and addresses the quality of an OAI's implementation. An effectiveness assessment includes MOEs and addresses the contribution of one OAI to advancement toward an objective. As with progress assessments, the design of performance and effectiveness assessments begins with identifying and refining objectives, which requires feedback from relevant stakeholders. After that, a planning process can determine the exact approach to pursue, and planners can develop a theory of change/logic model for it. A theory of change/logic model helps communicate the proposed connections between resources, activities, outputs, outcomes, and impacts. It allows planners to explicitly communicate implicit assumptions about an OAI, and it can guide measurement. Specifically, a theory of change/logic model encourages planners to consider which inputs they need to execute an effort, the actions they expect to take, the evidence needed to demonstrate that the actions were taken, and the short- and long-term changes that are expected to result from these actions.[2] Thus, after developing a theory of change/logic model, planners can choose nodes in the model to measure, collect and analyze data, and communicate results and recommendations to commanders and other stakeholders.

Although we have outlined essential processes in assessment design, applying the described frameworks for progress, performance, and effectiveness assessments might be challenging. Real-world implementation could reveal differences in understanding regarding objectives, gaps in information, and difficulties in measuring concepts of interest. However, engaging stakeholders, refining identified goals, and vetting theories of change can help move the various assessments in the direction of providing informative and actionable results and recommendations that commanders can use.

Recommendations

The following recommendations are intended to guide the actions and considerations of planners and practitioners.

Refine Approaches to Designing and Implementing Assessments

ECJ39 and broader working groups within USEUCOM should adopt the frameworks and processes for assessment design and implementation described in this report. The progress, performance, and effectiveness assessment frameworks will help USEUCOM planners and practitioners maintain a clear and systematic process for assessment design and ensure that they address the core components of an OAI whenever senior leadership requires a progress, performance, or effectiveness assessment.

---

[2] Paul et al., 2015.

Ensure That Sub-Objectives Are SMART

Planners and assessment practitioners should begin an assessment design by defining or refining sub-objectives so that they are SMART. Guidance, strategy, plans, or other communications might contain overlapping objectives that can be interpreted variously by diverse groups of stakeholders. Although it is challenging, planners must incorporate high-quality sub-objectives into assessment design. As discussed throughout this report, this often requires selecting one or a small set of objectives from a vast array of options and then defining or refining these sub-objectives to eliminate—or at least greatly reduce—ambiguities in wording and interpretation.

Involve Stakeholders in Assessment Design

Planners and assessment practitioners should engage relevant stakeholders throughout the assessment design process. To ensure that the results and recommendations from a progress, performance, or effectiveness assessment are useful to intended audiences, and to reduce the potential for confusion, feedback from relevant stakeholders should be sought at each step of an assessment's design. This report outlined some potential characteristics of this feedback process. Broadly speaking, in seeking stakeholder feedback, assessment planners and practitioners should provide clear guidance regarding what information they need to design and implement an assessment, why they need it, how they will use it, and when they will need it.

Determine the Suitability of Existing Data and the Need to Collect New Data to Support Assessment

Measures and indicators should clearly address identified objectives and underlying theories of change. Individuals or groups might currently collect various types of data on relevant topics. Rather than attempting to adjust the assessment design to incorporate currently collected data, planners and practitioners should first consider the extent to which these data and measures address selected objectives. Not all currently collected or available data or measures will be relevant to a particular progress, performance, or effectiveness assessment. New data or measures might be needed to better address the selected and refined sub-objectives.

Present Results in Ways That Are Most Useful to the Stakeholder

When communicating results, it is important to include information about the intent of the data collection and analysis, as well as recommendations for how specific stakeholders can use the assessment results. Rather than simply presenting a litany of results, it is better to provide commanders and other stakeholders with clear and actionable information that is organized in response to how they should or could use the results of each assessment—that is, provide answers to the "so what?" question. This will help reduce confusion regarding what to do with the information provided, thereby increasing the overall utility of the results.

Commanders: Ensure That Planners and Practitioners Have Sufficient Time and Resources

Our final recommendation applies to commanders. High-quality assessment design requires time and resources. Planners and assessment practitioners should receive sufficient time and resources to implement a well-designed progress, performance, or effectiveness assessment. It is unlikely that one individual will be able to independently design a high-quality and maximally informative evaluation in a highly restricted time frame. If the full benefits of an evaluation are to be recognized, the design and implementation of any type of assessment must be appropriately resourced.

Directions for Further Research

The assessment approaches, process guidance, and corresponding considerations described in this report suggest possible avenues for further research to enhance assessment processes and capabilities at USEUCOM and perhaps inform similar enhancements across DoD:

- Explore what data, information, and analyses ECJ39 and supporting components need and what data they already collect or otherwise receive. Consider the underlying objectives driving these various measurement efforts. Systematic collection and synthesis of this information can help identify gaps and potential duplication of effort.
- Investigate new data collection techniques and types of data that are being used elsewhere in DoD, the intelligence community, and other sectors. Consider how they might be applied to address different objectives—or categories of objectives—across USEUCOM.
- Review the characteristics and intent of relevant USEUCOM military exercises to identify overarching assumptions, including those regarding what deterrence is and how such exercises promote it. These reviews could point to a need for different or additional measures and analyses that could further assist USEUCOM in assessing the effects of these exercises.

References

Breedlove, Philip M., *United States European Command Theater Strategy*, Stuttgart, Germany: U.S. European Command, October 2015.

Center for Army Lessons Learned, *MDMP: Lessons and Best Practices*, No. 15-06, March 2015.

Curtis E. LeMay Center for Doctrine Development and Education, *The Joint Operation Planning Process for Air*, Maxwell Air Force Base, Ala., November 4, 2016. As of December 22, 2019: http://www.doctrine.af.mil/Portals/61/documents/Annex_3-0/3-0-D29-G-OPS-JOPPA.pdf

DoD—*See* U.S. Department of Defense.

Fishbein, Martin, and Icek Ajzen, *Belief, Attitude, Intention, and Behavior: An Introduction to Theory and Research*, Reading, Mass.: Addison-Wesley, 1975.

Gale, John, Stephenie Loux, and Andrew Coburn, *Creating Program Logic Models: A Toolkit for State Flex Programs*, Minneapolis, Minn., Chapel Hill, N.C., and Portland, Me.: Flex Monitoring Team, University of Minnesota, University of North Carolina, and University of Southern Maine, April 2006. As of December 22, 2019: https://www.flexmonitoring.org/wp-content/uploads/2013/07/PLMToolkit.pdf

Headquarters, U.S. Department of the Army, *Psychological Operations Leaders Planning Guide*, Graphic Training Aid 33-01-001, November 2005.

Huth, Paul K., "Deterrence and International Conflict: Empirical Findings and Theoretical Debates," *Annual Review of Political Science*, Vol. 2, June 1999, pp. 25–48.

Jablonski, Kathleen, and Mark Guagliardo, *Data Analysis Plans: A Blueprint for Success Using SAS*, Cary, N.C.: SAS Institute, 2016.

Joint Publication 3-0, *Joint Operations*, Washington, D.C.: U.S. Joint Chiefs of Staff, January 17, 2017.

Joint Publication 3-13, *Information Operations*, Washington, D.C.: U.S. Joint Chiefs of Staff, November 27, 2012, incorporating change 1, November 20, 2014.

Joint Publication 3-30, *Joint Air Operations*, Washington, D.C.: U.S. Joint Chiefs of Staff, July 25, 2019.

Joint Publication 5-0, *Joint Planning*, Washington, D.C.: U.S. Joint Chiefs of Staff, June 16, 2017.

JP—*See* Joint Publication.

Mazarr, Michael J., *Understanding Deterrence*, Santa Monica, Calif.: RAND Corporation, PE-295-RC, 2018. As of December 22, 2019: https://www.rand.org/pubs/perspectives/PE295.html

NATO—*See* North Atlantic Treaty Organization.

Newcomer, Kathryn E., Harry P. Hatry, and Joseph S. Wholey, "Planning and Designing Useful Evaluations," in Joseph S. Wholey, Harry P. Hatry, and Kathryn E. Newcomer, eds., *Handbook of Practical Program Evaluation*, 3rd ed., Hoboken, N.J.: Jossey-Bass, 2010, pp. 5–29.

North Atlantic Treaty Organization, "NATO Secretary General Briefs on Exercise Trident Juncture," October 24, 2018. As of December 22, 2019:
https://www.nato.int/cps/en/natohq/news_159663.htm

Paul, Christopher, *Assessing and Evaluating Department of Defense Efforts to Inform, Influence, and Persuade: Worked Example*, Santa Monica, Calif.: RAND Corporation, RR-809/4-OSD, 2017. As of December 22, 2019:
https://www.rand.org/pubs/research_reports/RR809z4.html

Paul, Christopher, and Miriam Matthews, *The Language of Inform, Influence, and Persuade: Assessment Lexicon and Usage Guide for U.S. European Command Efforts*, Santa Monica, Calif.: RAND Corporation, RR-2655-EUCOM, 2018. As of December 22, 2019:
https://www.rand.org/pubs/research_reports/RR2655.html

Paul, Christopher, Jessica Yeats, Colin P. Clarke, Miriam Matthews, and Lauren Skrabala, *Assessing and Evaluating Department of Defense Efforts to Inform, Influence, and Persuade: Handbook for Practitioners*, Santa Monica, Calif.: RAND Corporation, RR-809/2-OSD, 2015. As of December 22, 2019:
https://www.rand.org/pubs/research_reports/RR809z2.html

Shadish, William R., Thomas D. Cook, and Donald T. Campbell, *Experimental and Quasi-Experimental Designs for Generalized Causal Inference*, Boston, Mass.: Houghton Mifflin, 2001.

U.S. Department of Defense, *Deterrence Operations Joint Operating Concept, Version 2.0*, Washington, D.C., December 2006.

———, *Joint Concept for Operating in the Information Environment (JCOIE)*, Washington, D.C., July 25, 2018.